Core Knowledge®

ISBN: 978-1-68380-301-0

Early Presidents

Table of Contents

Early Presidents
Reader
Core Knowledge History and Geography™

Chapter 1
Washington Becomes President

Home at Mount Vernon The candles in the windows of George Washington's home at Mount Vernon shone brightly on Christmas Eve 1783, as they did every Christmas Eve. This Christmas Eve, though, was different. One month earlier the United States and Great Britain had signed a peace treaty ending the Revolutionary War.

The Big Question

Why was George Washington chosen to be the first president of the United States?

It was Christmastime when George Washington returned to his home. He was no longer the commander of the Continental Army.

f Washington, Mt. Vernon, Va.

Soon after, at a dinner in New York, General Washington said his goodbyes to his fellow officers. Later he presented Congress with his **resignation** as commander in chief of the Continental Army. His work was done, he told the Congress. He was retiring from public life forever—from the army, from government, from all the duties that America had called on him to do.

Washington had set an example for laying down his sword and surrendering his military authority to the people and the **republic** that represented them. He had done something no one else in history had done. King George III said that if he did that, "He would be the greatest man in the world."

Americans called Washington the "Father of His Country." They had a great deal of respect for their general. Some called him "Cincinnatus," after the legendary Roman general. Cincinnatus was given power by the Roman republic and then surrendered it. This was perhaps George Washington's greatest contribution to the founding of America.

Now, after nearly nine years of service to his country, Washington was free to return to his beloved Mount Vernon. As he rode up the circular drive to Mount Vernon that Christmas Eve, his wife, Martha, waited in the doorway to welcome him. At last, America's hero was home.

When Washington told Congress he was leaving public life forever, he meant it. Have you ever noticed, though, how sometimes things happen that make you take back words like *forever, never,* and *always*? That is what happened to George Washington.

First, Virginia asked him to **serve** as one of the state's **delegates** to the Constitutional Convention in Philadelphia. How could Washington say no? He had fought to give life to the young nation. But for the last four years, he could only watch helplessly as it struggled under the **Articles of Confederation**. He could not turn his back on his country. He had to take back that *forever*. He had to serve.

Vocabulary
....

serve, v. to work for one's country, as a government official or in the military

delegate, n. a representative

Articles of Confederation, n. the first plan of government of the United States; replaced by the U.S. Constitution in 1789

Then, the delegates to the Constitutional Convention gathered in Philadelphia in 1787. They needed a strong, steady leader to

George Washington was chosen to lead the Constitutional Convention.

get them through the hard work ahead. They turned to George Washington to serve as chairman of the convention.

Again, Washington agreed to serve.

And now, with the Constitution **ratified** by the states, Washington knew he would be called to serve again. As expected, he was

everyone's choice to be the nation's first president. Once again, he knew he could not say no. *Forever* would have to wait. He would serve the republic again to make sure the new nation got off to a good start.

On April 16, Washington said goodbye to Mount Vernon once again and set out for New York, the nation's temporary capital. There his inauguration would take place. An inauguration is a formal ceremony at the start of a term of office.

George Washington was sworn in as president on April 30, 1789.

The trip from Mount Vernon to New York City took far longer than Washington expected. In every village and town he traveled through, he had to attend speeches, parades, and dinners in his honor. Citizens lined the streets to cheer as his carriage passed by. On the country roads, men on horseback rode in front of, behind, and alongside Washington's carriage. The traffic filled the country air with dust as the journey became one long parade. After eight days, Washington finally arrived in New York.

Inauguration Day—April 30, 1789—dawned bright and sunny in New York City. A crowd of thousands assembled in front of the building known as Federal Hall. Shortly after noon, George Washington and a small group of officials stepped out on the balcony. Placing his hand on a Bible, Washington repeated the **oath of office** written in the new Constitution: "I do solemnly swear that I will faithfully execute the office of President of the United States, and will to the best of my ability, preserve, protect, and defend the Constitution of the United States."

> **Vocabulary**
>
> **oath of office,** n. a promise made by a government official to obey the law and fulfill the responsibilities of his or her job

Because there were no loudspeakers in 1789, few people on the street below could hear the words. Nevertheless, they knew they had witnessed a historic moment. After Washington spoke the final words of the oath, an official called out, "Long live George Washington, President of the United States!" The crowd cheered wildly.

Chapter 2
The First Year

Setting Precedents With the election of a congress and a president, the new government was ready to start. Washington and Congress wanted to proceed carefully because, as Washington said, "I walk on untrodden ground." He meant that no one had ever done anything like this before.

The Big Question
....
What steps did the First Congress take to help establish a more organized system of government?

Vocabulary
....
precedent, n. an example for future actions or decisions

Almost every action they took might set a **precedent**. That is, every action they took might set a pattern that would be followed in the future. Washington wanted to set the right precedents by closely following the Constitution in carrying out his duties as president and protecting the liberties of the people.

For example, members of Congress tied themselves into knots over the proper way to address the president. Vice President John Adams suggested that the president be called, "His Highness, the President of the United States of America and Protector of Their Liberties." Others said that sounded too much like the way a king is addressed.

As the first U.S. president, George Washington set the precedent, or example, for other presidents to follow.

Some thought "His Excellency" was the right way. In the end it was agreed to address Washington simply as "Mr. President." Today, the matter seems more amusing than important. But in 1789, it was taken very seriously.

Other precedents were more important. For example, the Constitution set up three branches of government: the **legislative**, **judicial**, and **executive** branches. The Constitution also said there will be "departments" in the executive branch of government to help the president. It does not say, though, what those departments will be. It also does not say how many of them there will be. It was up to Congress to fill in that empty space in the Constitution.

Congress decided to create three executive departments. One was the Department of State. That department was supposed to help the president in his dealings with foreign countries. Another department was the Department of War. That department was in charge of defending the country. A third department was the Department of the Treasury. That one was expected to collect **taxes**, pay bills, and take care of the government's money. The head of each department was called a *secretary*.

Creating these departments led to another precedent. The Constitution says the president may seek advice from his department heads. At first, Washington just talked to each secretary separately about the work his department was doing. After a while, though, President Washington felt he needed advice on many other matters. He began having all the secretaries meet with him at the same time to get their advice. The department heads came to be called the president's *Cabinet*, which means a group of advisers. The first Cabinet also included an attorney general, who gave the president legal advice, and a postmaster general, who ran the post office. The meetings came to be known as *Cabinet meetings*.

The Constitution does not say anything about a Cabinet. Every president since Washington, though, has had one. Over the years,

Although it is not in the Constitution, every president has had a Cabinet to advise him. This was George Washington's Cabinet.

Congress has added departments to the executive branch, and the president's Cabinet has grown.

Another of those empty spaces in the Constitution had to do with the courts. The Constitution says that there will be a Supreme Court. It does not say how many judges should serve on it. It says that Congress can establish courts below the Supreme Court. It does not say what those courts should do or how many there should be. All of that was up to Congress.

Therefore, in that very first year under the new government, Congress passed a law filling in details about courts and judges. It said the Supreme Court should have six judges. Congress changed that number several times over the years. Sometimes it was seven, then eight, then nine, then ten, then eight again, and nine again! (It has been nine for more than 130 years, so it will probably stay that way. But that is not to say that it cannot change again. It is possible, as the court is not constitutionally bound to nine members.) The Supreme Court, of course, is the top court in the country. Congress, however, also created enough other courts so that people in every part of the country could use the court system.

A United States Tax

During that first year, Congress passed another important law regarding the government. In the old days, the central government did not have any money. The government also owed about $79 million, including debt from the Revolutionary War. That was because the government did not have the power to tax. The new

Constitution changed that. In 1789, Congress placed a tax on more than eighty imported products—that is, products brought into the United States from other countries. It was not much of a tax, but it was enough. For the first time, the central government could start paying its bills.

The greatest success of the First Congress, however, was passing a **Bill of Rights**. James Madison was the author of these first ten amendments. He urged his fellow representatives to pass the Bill of Rights. They agreed, and the basic liberties of the people became the law of the land when the states ratified the Bill of Rights.

The First Congress added the Bill of Rights to the Constitution.

Chapter 3
Hamilton and Jefferson

A Solid Foundation What a busy year 1789 was for the new government of the United States! New executive departments. A brand new federal court system. Important precedents. The new nation's first-ever tax.

The Big Question

How did Hamilton's and Jefferson's beliefs about government differ?

In just six months, President Washington and Congress had laid a solid foundation for a healthy new government.

What is more, the American people seemed very satisfied. Less than a year earlier, arguments about the Constitution had raged in the state ratifying conventions. Now, wrote Thomas Jefferson, "the opposition to our new Constitution has almost totally disappeared."

Vocabulary

administration, n. a group of people responsible for carrying out the day-to-day workings of an organization

But the harmony did not last. Differences soon arose among Washington's closest advisers and Congress. The differences grew into angry debates. Before long they threatened to tear apart Washington's **administration**.

Even among George Washington's close advisers there was conflict.

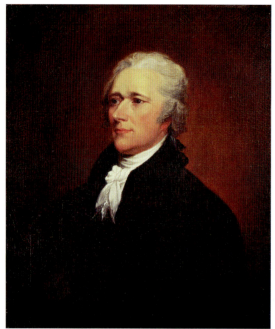

Alexander Hamilton (left) and Thomas Jefferson (right) disagreed on almost everything.

At the very start of his administration, President Washington had chosen Alexander Hamilton to head the Department of the Treasury. He chose Thomas Jefferson to head the Department of State. Hamilton and Jefferson were two of the most capable people ever to serve in government. They were both great patriots. But they disagreed on almost everything. At times, President Washington felt as if he were driving a coach with horses pulling in opposite directions.

Scholars believe that the two men had never met before Washington appointed them to his Cabinet. James Madison, who knew both men well, introduced them to each other. Madison thought they would get along just fine. Was he ever wrong! In just a few months, conflict between the two men grew.

Different Hopes for the Nation

Hamilton and Jefferson had almost completely opposite hopes and plans for America's future. Hamilton supported farming. But, he also wanted to encourage the growth of manufacturing for a **diverse** economy. He pictured great numbers of Americans being employed at machines, producing goods for sale in America and other countries. Jefferson agreed that the country needed some manufacturing and trade. However, he wanted America to remain mostly a nation of small farmers.

Hamilton hoped the United States would have many large cities. Jefferson did not want to see cities grow. He had seen Europe's large cities, with their masses of poor and hungry people. He wanted no part of that for America.

Hamilton favored a strong, energetic, central government tied to powerful business interests. This, he thought, would help to create a strong, **stable** country. Jefferson said, "That government governs best, which governs least." That is, the smaller the government, the better. He believed that a nation of farmers and small businesses would guarantee people economic independence and liberty.

Who should run this government and make decisions? Here again, Hamilton and Jefferson came down on opposite sides. For Hamilton, government should be in the hands of "the rich, the well-born, and the able." *Well-born* means they should come from important, aristocratic families. These people, he said, would be more experienced and more able to make wise decisions. This does not mean that Hamilton believed that ordinary people could not govern. Instead he thought the experience needed to govern well came from certain groups or types of people.

Jefferson, though, believed that ordinary people could be and should be involved in governing themselves. "Whenever the people are well-informed" he wrote, "they can be trusted with their own government."

One thing that Alexander Hamilton did that helped kick-start America's economy was to create the First Bank of the United States. It was a national bank. This step allowed for the creation of a common **currency**. Once again, this development was not welcomed by all.

> **Vocabulary**
>
> **currency,** n. a system of money

With such opposite beliefs, it's no wonder that Hamilton and Jefferson disliked each other so strongly. In fact, each one regarded the other as dangerous to the future of the young republic. They were wrong about that. Both contributed greatly to the nation's growth and health in its early years.

The many disagreements between Hamilton and Jefferson led to the birth of political parties in America. A political party is a group of people who share certain beliefs about how the government should be run and what it should and should not do. These people join together to elect representatives who share their beliefs.

In the 1790s, those Americans who favored Hamilton and his ideas called themselves *Federalists*. Supporters of Thomas Jefferson called themselves *Democratic-Republicans*.

The Whiskey Rebellion

Congress still needed money to pay the nation's debts. Alexander Hamilton proposed a solution. Hamilton's idea was to raise money by Congress putting a tax on certain goods, including whiskey. People disagreed with other parts of Hamilton's plan. However, almost everyone thought the tax on whiskey was reasonable and constitutional. Congress passed it by a majority **vote**, and the president signed the bill into law.

> **Vocabulary**
>
> **vote,** n. an official choice made by a person through casting a ballot, raising a hand, or speaking aloud
>
> **frontier,** n. where newly settled areas meet unsettled, but not necessarily uninhabited, areas

Although almost everyone thought the tax was fair, certain settlers on the western **frontier** thought it was unreasonable. Many of those farmers raised corn as their main crop. Although farm families used most of what they grew to live on, they planned to sell the remainder. But the cost of shipping corn to eastern cities by wagon added so much to its price that few buyers could be found for it.

Whiskey can be made from corn. Shipping a barrel of whiskey cost less than shipping the corn it was made from. So farmers often turned their corn into whiskey.

For these farmers, paying a tax on whiskey was like paying a tax on the corn itself. Money was scarce on the frontier. Frontier farmers often used jugs of whiskey as a substitute. For farmers who used whiskey that way, taxing whiskey was like taxing money itself!

In 1794, farmers in western Pennsylvania banded together and refused to pay the tax. They felt that the tax challenged their rights, especially since they believed the national government was not properly representing their needs and concerns. They believed it was another case of "no taxation without representation." They even threatened and physically harmed tax collectors. President Washington had some sympathy for the farmers. But he felt that the law must be followed. He also felt it was especially important for the new government to show it could enforce its laws. Washington put on his old general's uniform and led

This illustration shows a group of whiskey rebels with a tarred and feathered tax collector.

thirteen thousand troops to western Pennsylvania to put down the Whiskey Rebellion, as it was called.

Happily, no one fired a shot. When farmers heard that troops were coming, they dropped their guns and fled. A couple of the leaders were tried and convicted. But Washington pardoned them. That ended the rebellion. Washington had shown that the new government could not only pass laws, but also make people obey them.

Still, the use of troops to put down the Whiskey Rebellion left a bitter taste in the mouths of many farmers. It also demonstrated the power of the new national government and its willingness to use it. The farmers turned against the Federalist Party. They knew that Jefferson supported farmers. So, they gave their support to the Democratic-Republican Party.

Chapter 4
The First Adams

A New President Twice the American people had chosen George Washington to be their president. Twice he had served, even though he would rather have returned to his beloved Mount Vernon. If Americans had their way, Washington would go right on serving as president.

The time had come for a new president to be chosen. The election of 1796 was the first election in which political parties played a role.

John Adams

Washington, however, decided that eight years as president was enough. Not just enough for him, but enough for the country. He believed that if the new government was to succeed, the people

must not depend on just one man. America needed a president, not a king. Once again, Washington voluntarily surrendered power back to the republic and the people. He returned to his home at Mount Vernon. In doing this, he set the precedent of presidents serving only two terms in office. This was not a constitutional rule but a **moral** precedent that was intended to prevent a return to being ruled by a monarch. Presidents followed Washington's example for 140 years!

With Washington out of the picture, the United States had its first real contest for the presidency. John Adams, who had been Washington's vice president, was the candidate of the Federalist Party. The Democratic-Republicans named Thomas Jefferson as their choice for president. John Adams won, but just barely.

In those days, the person who came in second became the vice president, even though he might be from the other political party. So Thomas Jefferson became vice president of the United States. This method of election was soon changed by the Twelfth Amendment to the Constitution.

John Adams was a greatly respected American. But he was not loved as Washington was. And he was not especially popular. While he was president, he had to make a decision that made him even less popular. But it was the right decision for the country.

An Old Problem

The problem had actually begun while Washington was still president. Those old enemies, France and Great Britain, were back at war again. During the U.S. War for Independence, France had been America's best friend. The French navy and army had made possible the victory at Yorktown, which ended the war.

Now the French thought that it was America's turn to help them fight Great Britain. Some Americans agreed. Many favored France because the French people had just had a revolution of their own. They had overthrown their king and set up a republic. Many of the Americans who wanted to help France were Democratic-Republicans.

During the French Revolution, the king was removed from power.

Other Americans, however, thought the United States should side with Great Britain. Most people who felt this way were Federalists. President Washington decided that the United States must remain neutral, which means it would not take sides. It would stay out of the fighting.

Even when the British navy began to seize American ships and sailors carrying goods to France, Washington was determined to keep the United States out of war. He knew that the young nation needed time to grow and become stronger. He feared that war might destroy the modern world's first great experiment with republican government.

John Adams also believed it was important to keep the United States out of war. However, by the time he became president, that was even more difficult. By then, the French navy had also started seizing the ships of American merchants. At the same time, the French government was threatening the United States. President Adams hoped to keep America at peace. He sent three personal representatives to France to ask the French to stop. But French officials insisted on a large loan to France before they would even talk to the Americans. The Americans returned empty-handed and angry.

In response to the French, Congress created a navy department and paid for the building of a number of ships. It looked like war for sure.

A Tough Decision

President Adams knew that taking military action would make him popular. But like President Washington before him, he also knew that the young republic needed peace. He decided he must try once more to find another solution. He sent a new ambassador to France. This time the French government talked with the American ambassador, and the two reached an agreement. President Adams had done the right thing. He had kept America out of a war. But in doing so, he lost a lot of popular support. Federalists who had wanted to go to war turned against him. Democratic-Republicans were not going to support him anyway.

President Adams was also involved in a battle about the power of the federal government. He signed a series of laws that made it more difficult for foreigners to become American citizens. It also became a crime to criticize the government. These laws were unpopular among Democratic-Republicans. Adams found himself in a very difficult situation.

Chapter 5
A New Capital for the New Nation

Federal City Here is a puzzler to stump your friends with: What do the following cities have in common— Philadelphia, Pennsylvania; Lancaster, Pennsylvania; York, Pennsylvania; Princeton, New Jersey; Trenton, New Jersey; Annapolis, Maryland; and New York, New York?

The Big Question
....
How did Washington, D.C., become the capital of the United States?

The answer? Each city was once the capital of the United States of America. Several served as the capital during the War for Independence. Several others served during the days of the Articles of Confederation. In each of those cities today, you will find a historical marker proudly stating that it was once the capital. The truth is, though, that when the government was weak and unimportant, none of those places cared much about being the capital.

However, once the new Constitution set up a strong national government, people cared very much about the location of the capital. New York, where President Washington took the oath of office, was just a temporary capital.

New York City was only a temporary capital when George Washington became president.

The Constitution expected that a state, or several states, would give the new government a chunk of land for a permanent capital. Several states offered land. They wanted to have the capital nearby because many businesses and visitors would come to their state.

In 1790, Congress accepted an offer of land from Maryland and Virginia. The land was near the middle of the states that then made up the United States. Congress also made Philadelphia the temporary capital for the next ten years, while the new capital was being built.

President Washington chose the exact piece of land, which was to be called the Territory of Columbia. (It is now known as the District of Columbia.) The president selected a site across the Potomac River from his own home at Mount Vernon. The plan was for the government building to be located in one part of the district. That part was called the Federal City or the City of Washington. Later on, it all came to be known as Washington, District of Columbia, or Washington, D.C.

Designing the City

President Washington hired a well-known surveyor, Andrew Ellicott, to map out the area. Ellicott needed a scientific assistant for this work, someone who knew a lot about mathematics. He chose a self-taught African American named Benjamin Banneker.

> **Vocabulary**
>
> **surveyor,** n.
> a person who measures the shape, size, and features of an area of land

Together, Ellicott and Banneker surveyed the district, noting every feature of the land.

To design the Federal City, President Washington hired an engineer named Pierre L'Enfant (/pyer/lahn*fahn/). He was a French army officer who had fought with the Continental Army. He first met George Washington at Valley Forge.

L'Enfant was a brilliant engineer and **architect** (/ahr*kuh*tekt/). Unfortunately, he had a terrible temper. He always had to have his way. This got him in trouble with a lot of people, including Washington and Jefferson. L'Enfant was fired less than a year into the job.

During that time, though, L'Enfant used Ellicott and Banneker's survey to lay out the basic plan for the city of Washington. He adopted Jefferson's idea for a grid system for the city's streets. A grid system looks like the lines on a checkerboard. Then he added several broad avenues that spread out from the center, like spokes on a wheel. His plan set aside spaces for the main government buildings. The Capitol would be set on a hill. (*Capitol* is the building where the members of the Senate and the House of Representatives meet. The word *capital* refers to the city.) The "President's Palace" was to be located on lower ground, with a fine view of the Potomac River. (The President's Palace was later called the President's House, and still later, the White House.) L'Enfant also reserved open spaces for parks, monuments, and fountains. It was a beautiful plan.

Designing the Buildings

After L'Enfant left, the government decided to hold contests for the best designs for the Capitol and for the President's Palace.

By 1800, the Capitol and the White House were ready for Congress and the president.

The winners presented handsome drawings of what the buildings should look like, but they did not know how to draw the actual construction plans. Before those buildings came to look like they do today, many other people would contribute their ideas, and many more years would pass.

Nevertheless, by 1800, those buildings, and several others, were ready enough to be used. So in that year, right on schedule, the government moved from Philadelphia to its new home.

A few people had bought land in the part known as the Federal City or Washington. They built homes, **boardinghouses**, and other places of business. They were looking ahead to the time when the government

would move there. But the buildings were far apart, and there were tree stumps everywhere. None of the roads were paved. You can imagine what they were like when it rained.

An Uncomfortable Home

President Adams and his family moved into the President's House in November 1800. We don't have to guess what the Adams family thought about their new home. We have the letters that Abigail Adams, the president's wife, wrote to members of her family. Abigail Adams reported that on the day they arrived, not a single room had been completely finished. In some rooms, the plaster walls were still damp. The main staircase to the second floor was also unfinished. Abigail Adams turned one of the large

Abigail Adams saw great potential in the White House and in the new nation.

unfinished rooms into a laundry room where the family wash was hung to dry.

This was before the days of **furnaces**. People depended on fireplaces for warmth. There was a fireplace in each room of the President's House to take the chill off and

keep the house dry. That was fine, but nobody had thought to supply firewood. It turned out that the president was responsible for supplying his own. There was also no well for water. Servants had to carry water from a distance of five city blocks.

Still, Abigail Adams found much to like about the house. She could see its possibilities, as she could see the possibilities for the young republic. Unfinished? Yes, they both were. But Abigail was sure the new house, like the new nation, would become great. She knew this house was not built for a year or a decade. She wrote to her sister, "This House is built for ages to come."

Chapter 6
The Many-Sided Jefferson

Fighting and Name Calling When Adams ran for reelection to the presidency, he lost. Unfortunately, the election of 1800 was filled with fighting and name-calling between the two parties. The new president was none other than the leader of the Democratic-Republicans, Thomas Jefferson.

The Big Question

What important changes did Thomas Jefferson make to the country during his presidency?

Vocabulary

Electoral College, n. a group of representatives who elect the president and vice president, based on the popular vote in each state

Soon after Thomas Jefferson became president, all of the following lived in the White House: an architect, a lawyer, a scholar, an inventor, an author, a scientific farmer, and a politician. Can you guess how many people lived in the White House?

Thomas Jefferson barely beat another Democratic-Republican, Aaron Burr. Jefferson and Burr tied in the Electoral College, and the House of Representatives decided the election as allowed by the Constitution. Aaron Burr became vice president.

The answer is one—Thomas Jefferson. You see, Jefferson was all those things. Like his countryman, Benjamin Franklin, Jefferson was a man of endless curiosity. He was a **philosopher**. He owned more than 6,500 books, on almost every subject imaginable. His book collection became the start of the collection for the Library of Congress!

Like Franklin, Jefferson applied a scientific approach to everything. All his life he recorded his observations of the weather, the stars, and the world of nature around him. On his plantation he continually experimented to discover which plants and trees from around the world would grow well in Virginia. He even wrote a book about his state's animal and plant life and its geography.

While still in his early twenties, Jefferson designed and supervised the construction of his home and of everything in it, right down to the furniture and curtains. The house sits on a mountaintop in central Virginia, so Jefferson called it *Monticello*. The word is Italian for "little mountain." Over the years, he invented many gadgets for Monticello that still delight the thousands who visit there each year. Later, Jefferson designed the campus and the first buildings of the University of Virginia.

Jefferson believed that "the pursuit of happiness" was only possible when the rights and freedoms of ordinary people were protected. According to Jefferson, this was only possible when they governed themselves. Jefferson's faith in ordinary people, though, came with one very big condition: the people must

Jefferson designed almost every aspect of his home at Monticello.

be educated. He believed an ignorant and uneducated people would never remain free for long. Years before Jefferson became president, he tried to get his state of Virginia to provide free education. But this idea was too advanced for people at that time. Jefferson's attempt was unsuccessful. Of course, at the time, only free, white property-owning males were in a position to benefit from Jefferson's beliefs.

Sadly, Jefferson also failed to persuade his state to accept another of his ideas. Jefferson viewed slavery as evil. He tried to get Virginia to pass a law that children born to enslaved people would be automatically free at birth. Jefferson also drafted the 1784 Land Ordinance that would have banned slavery in all western states. It lost in Congress by only one vote. It was not to be. In 1807, the government did agree on a bill to end the slave trade. Jefferson signed this bill into law.

Yet Jefferson himself owned many enslaved people, as nearly every well-to-do Southern family did. Jefferson had an interesting exchange of letters on the subject of slavery with Benjamin Banneker, a free African American who helped to build the Federal City. Banneker reminded Jefferson of his own words in the Declaration of Independence—that all men are created equal, and that one of their **unalienable** rights is liberty. Why then, Banneker asked, was slavery allowed to continue? And how could Jefferson himself continue to hold enslaved people?

In his reply, Jefferson agreed that slavery was wrong. He said that Banneker himself was proof that African Americans could achieve much, if given their freedom. But

> **Vocabulary**
>
> **unalienable,** adj.
> unable to be taken
> away or denied

he had no good answers to Banneker's questions. He especially had no good answers about his own enslaved people. Like many landowners of the time, Jefferson continued the practice of slavery, putting off the fight that would happen years later.

Mr. President

This is the man who prepared to take the office of president of the United States on March 4, 1801. That morning, Jefferson rose early as usual, wrote letters, and read in his room at a Washington, D.C., boardinghouse. He had breakfast with the other guests, as he had done for many days before. He was dressed in a plain suit, like those worn by plain citizens.

Shortly before noon, Thomas Jefferson stepped out of the boardinghouse, where he was met by a small group of officials.

Together they walked briskly through the muddy streets to the Capitol, where Jefferson would take the oath of office. No elegant uniform. No special badges. No ceremonial sword at his side. No elegant horse-drawn coach to carry him. No big parade. That was Thomas Jefferson.

That was Jefferson's White House, too. All visitors were treated the same. The British ambassador was offended that the president of the United States greeted him in slippers. At dinner, there was no special seating plan for guests. The first people to the table, whoever they might be, could sit next to the president if they wished. When Jefferson had to go anywhere outside the President's House, he rode on horseback by himself. There was no splendid presidential coach and no guards. President Jefferson did these things because he wanted to make a point. In a republic, all are equal. No one should have privileges above anyone else.

The Louisiana Purchase

President Jefferson and the members of his Democratic-Republican Party in Congress quickly changed many of the laws the Federalists had made. They got rid of the hated whiskey tax. They cut government spending. For example, they reduced the size of the army and the navy.

Jefferson had planned to make all the changes when he became president, so no one was surprised by them. His greatest achievement, however, was one he hadn't planned on at all. In fact, it came about through an incredible stroke of luck. Because he acted quickly when this situation arose, President Jefferson was able to double the size of the United States.

Back in the 1700s, France had claimed all the land between the Mississippi River and the Rocky Mountains. France called this area Louisiana, after King Louis of France. After one of its wars with Great Britain, France gave Louisiana to Spain.

To American farmers who lived in the West, the most important part of Louisiana was the port city of New Orleans, near the mouth of the Mississippi River. When you look at a map, you see why. If you were a western farmer growing corn or wheat, how would you send your crops to markets in the eastern cities or in Europe? Not by wagon. That would be far too expensive. You would put

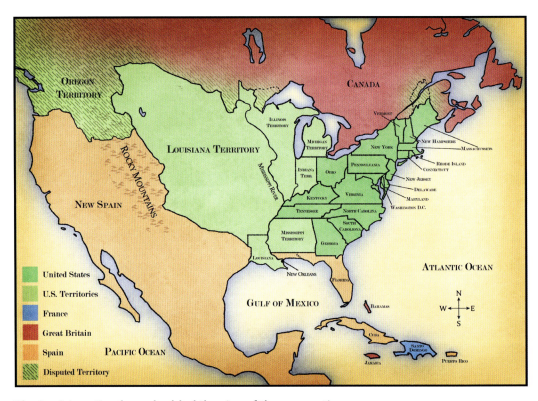

The Louisiana Purchase doubled the size of the new nation.

them on rafts and float them down rivers. All the rivers in that part of the country eventually flow into the Mississippi River. So New Orleans would be the end of the line for your crops. There you would sell them to a merchant, who would then put them on ships bound for the eastern cities, or Europe, or perhaps the West Indies.

What would happen, though, if the country that owned New Orleans stopped allowing Americans to use it? American farmers would not be able to get their crops to market. They would go broke.

In 1802, it looked like that might happen. Spain suddenly announced that western farmers could no longer use New Orleans. Even worse, President Jefferson learned that Spain had secretly given back all of Louisiana, including New Orleans, to France. Jefferson knew

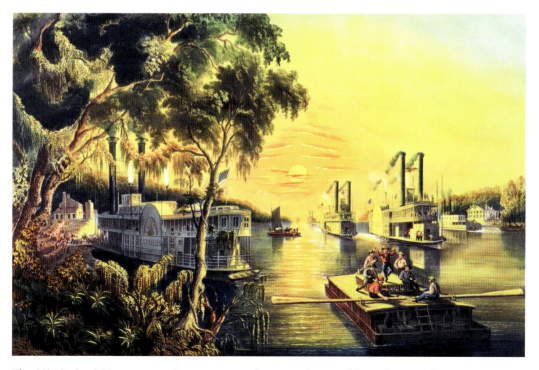

The Mississippi River was an important trade route that could not be cut off.

that the French emperor, Napoleon Bonaparte (/nuh*poh*lee*un/ boh*nuh*pahrt/), wanted to build a new empire in the Americas. This was serious trouble.

Jefferson sent two representatives to France and instructed them to offer $10 million for New Orleans. Here is where luck entered the picture. You remember how France and Great Britain were always going to war against each other? Well, they were about to do that again. France needed money. Also, Napoleon had given up his idea of a new French empire in North America.

When the American representatives offered France $10 million for New Orleans, they were amazed by France's reply. No, said the French, we're not interested in selling New Orleans by itself. But if you'd like to buy all of the Louisiana Territory, including New Orleans, for $15 million, we can make a deal.

The Americans quickly accepted. The Louisiana Purchase, as it was called, doubled America's territory at a cost of a few pennies an acre. It was the biggest bargain in American history.

Neither Jefferson nor anyone else knew exactly what he had bought. No one could know that until explorers went to see for themselves. They soon did. But that is a story for another time.

French leader Napoleon Bonaparte sold Louisiana to the United States so he could pay for a war with Great Britain.

Chapter 7
"Mr. Madison's War"

War in Europe You will not be surprised to learn that soon after the Louisiana Purchase, France and Britain were at war again. Once again the United States was determined not to get involved. But that was very hard to do.

The Big Question

Why did the United States go to war with Britain in 1812?

Soon after the Louisiana Purchase, the United States got caught up in a war between Great Britain and France.

The United States, you see, had already become an important trading nation. Both France and Great Britain were eager to buy American goods. That was fine with the United States. But each side wanted to keep the other from buying our goods. That was not fine with us. France said it would seize any ship trading with Great Britain, and Great Britain said it would seize any ship trading with France. Soon both the British and the French navies were capturing American ships.

That was bad enough. But the British also did something worse. Sometimes they took American sailors off American **merchant ships** and forced them to serve in the British navy. Why would the British want Americans to serve in their navy? Because conditions on a British naval ship were terrible, and captains were often cruel. A lot of British sailors took any opportunity to desert, or run away. As a result, the British navy was short of sailors.

Many of those British deserters took jobs on American merchant ships. The British captains wanted to get those men back. Can you see what is coming? The British navy began stopping American merchant ships to search for deserters. Sometimes by accident and sometimes on purpose, the British carried off American as well as British seamen. This practice was called **impressment**.

> ## Vocabulary
>
> **merchant ship,** n. a ship that transports goods for sale or trade
>
> **impressment,** n. the act of seizing seamen to serve against their will as sailors in a navy

You can imagine how angry Americans were about impressment. It reminded them of Britain's forceful rule of the colonies. They demanded that their government do something. Even if it meant war.

War was the last thing that President Jefferson wanted. There must be some other way to make Britain and France stop seizing our ships and our seamen, he thought. The idea he hit upon was this: stop trading. Stop trading altogether. Do not allow any ships—neither ours nor any other country's—to leave American ports, and do not permit any ships to enter them.

Such a complete stopping of trade is called an **embargo**. Jefferson proposed that the embargo would continue until Great Britain and France agreed to leave U.S. ships alone. You see, Jefferson believed that those

> ### Vocabulary
> **embargo,** n. a government order that limits or stops trade

countries needed American trade so badly that they would have to agree to stop seizing our ships. Congress thought the idea was a good one, and the embargo began.

Jefferson did not expect what happened next. The embargo wound up hurting Americans more than it hurt Great Britain and France. American merchants, a majority of whom were Federalists, could not sell their goods. Farmers could not sell their crops. Shipbuilders lost business. Sailors lost jobs. Americans hated the embargo. And worst of all, Great Britain and France did not promise to change.

The embargo was a failure. After one year, Congress repealed, or canceled, the embargo law. Ships once again entered and left American ports. The British and French went right back to seizing American ships, and the British impressed American sailors again. Nothing had changed.

Madison for Peace

By this time, Thomas Jefferson's term in office had ended, and a new president was in the White House: James Madison.

People were already calling Madison the "Father of the Constitution" because of his contributions to the Constitutional Convention. He had served in the Congress for many years. He had helped get the Bill of Rights added to the Constitution. He had helped Thomas Jefferson form the Democratic-Republican Party. He had served as Jefferson's **secretary of state**.

As president, Madison was no more successful than Jefferson had been in dealing with Great Britain and France. Once, France tricked him into believing that they would leave our ships alone. Madison wanted so badly to believe the French that even after everyone else saw they were not keeping their word, Madison still said they were.

Americans were angry at France, but they were even angrier at Great Britain. Great Britain not only seized American ships, but they also impressed American sailors. They were also angry because

James Madison was reluctant to have the United States declare war on Great Britain.

50

in the Northwest Territory, Native Americans were attacking American settlements, killing some settlers and driving away others. Why should Americans blame Great Britain for that? Because the Native Americans were getting their guns from the British government in Canada. Some westerners thought the only way to stop the attacks was to drive the British out of Canada.

Congress talked more and more about war with Great Britain. Some congressmen said the United States must defend its honor against the British navy. There were even people who wanted the United States to have Canada for itself and were willing to go to war to get it.

Congressmen who talked this way became known as the War Hawks. Most of them were younger men who had not fought in the American Revolution, or in the various wars fought against Native Americans. Some had not even been born when the War for Independence happened. These men did not know—at least not from their own experience—how terrible war can be. To them, war was all about glory. They were eager to fight. It would all be so easy, they thought. Why, the Kentucky **militia** could take Canada all by itself, said one of them. (He was from Kentucky, of course!)

> **Vocabulary**
>
> **militia,** n. a group of armed citizens prepared for military service at any time

War Is Declared

Older Americans, such as James Madison, knew more about war. They really hoped to avoid it. In the end, the pressure from his own party was too much for President Madison. In 1812, he asked Congress to declare war against Great Britain. Congress quickly did. Those who opposed the war called it "Mr. Madison's War."

You might think that if a country plans to go to war, it would at least prepare for it. The United States, though, was almost completely unprepared. American leaders talked about taking on the British navy with its six hundred ships, while the U.S. navy had only sixteen. U.S. leaders talked about driving the British out of Canada, while the U.S. army had only seven thousand soldiers.

It is not surprising, then, that at first things did not go well for Americans in the West. American troops not only failed to take Canada but also were forced to surrender some American land.

Then came a big surprise: America's first victory came on water rather than on land. The United States had a small fleet on Lake Erie, one of the Great Lakes. Great Britain had a larger one. The American fleet was commanded by Oliver H. Perry. Perry was only twenty-eight years old, but he had served in the navy since he was fourteen. In September 1813, Perry's fleet defeated a British naval force on Lake Erie, forcing it to surrender. Perry then sent this message to the American general in the region: "We have met the enemy and they are ours."

The American fleet defeated the British fleet on Lake Erie.

The Burning of Washington

The next year, 1814, started out badly for the Americans. Great Britain's main enemy had always been France. But in 1814, the French armies surrendered to the British. That was not good news for the United States. It meant that the British could now turn their full attention to fighting Americans.

That summer, a British fleet sailed into Chesapeake Bay in Maryland with several thousand troops. Their mission was to destroy the American capital city, Washington, D.C.

Residents of Washington fled into the countryside, ahead of the arrival of the British troops. But Dolley Madison, the president's wife, coolly remained at the White House until she had arranged to save important government records and a fine painting of George Washington. Only then did she and the last of the White House guards leave. She left just hours before the redcoats arrived!

When British soldiers burst into the empty White House, they found a dinner that had been prepared for the Madisons. British officers enjoyed the fine food. Then the troops went through the place, destroying everything in their path. Finally, they set fire to the White House, the Capitol, and many other government buildings. The next day, a hurricane hit Washington, adding to the damage. Luckily, the heavy rainstorm that followed put out most of the fires.

In 1814, British troops burned Washington, D.C.

From Washington, the British marched to Baltimore. At the same time, the British fleet bombarded Fort McHenry, at the entrance to Baltimore's harbor. The

attack lasted all day and all night. But the Americans held out. That attack inspired Francis Scott Key to write the U.S. national anthem, the "Star-Spangled Banner."

O say, can you see,

by the dawn's early light,

What so proudly we hail'd

at the twilight's last gleaming?

Whose broad stripes and bright stars,

thro' the perilous fight,

O'er the **ramparts** we watch'd

were so gallantly streaming?

And the rockets' red glare,

the bombs bursting in air,

Gave proof thro' the night

that our flag was still there.

O say, does that star-spangled banner yet wave

O'er the land of the free

and the home of the brave?

The British attack on Fort McHenry inspired the writing of the U.S. national anthem.

The Battle of New Orleans

Near the end of 1814, the British tried to capture the city of New Orleans, at the mouth of the Mississippi River. A British fleet landed 7,500 soldiers near the city. General Andrew Jackson, commanding

a tough band of five thousand militia and **frontiersmen**, was waiting to meet them.

Pirates also helped defend New Orleans. Jean Lafitte was the leader of a band of pirates. Lafitte persuaded General Jackson to use his men and their cannons against the British.

The last attack of the battle began on January 8, 1815. Wave after wave of redcoats attacked the American defenses. Each wave was thrown back, with heavy losses to the British. After the defeat, the British retreated to their ships and left.

The War Is Over

The Battle of New Orleans was the final battle of the War of 1812. In fact, it actually took place *after* the war officially ended. News traveled so slowly in those days that the two armies did not know that their governments had signed a peace treaty two weeks earlier!

In that peace treaty, each side kept the same territory it had before the war. So one way of looking at the outcome of the war is that neither side won.

That is true. Neither side did win. But the Americans did have some gains to show for it all. They had shown themselves and the world that even if they could not defeat mighty Great Britain, they could certainly hold their own. In addition, the British stopped providing guns to Native Americans in the West. That was one of the goals of the United States. So all in all, the United States could feel satisfied with the outcome of the war.

However, Native Americans at this time did not feel as satisfied. For them, the war and the end of British support broke the back of their resistance to American settlement and expansion in the West. They lost important leaders and many warriors. The rise of this young nation was at the same time threatening the survival of Native American people who had lived on American soil for hundreds of years—long before European explorers had ventured across the Atlantic Ocean.

Chapter 8
Monroe and the Second Adams

James Monroe Have you noticed that, except for John Adams of Massachusetts, all of America's early presidents came from the state of Virginia? The man who followed James Madison in the presidency was another Virginian. His name was James Monroe.

The Big Question
....
Why did James Monroe put the Monroe Doctrine in place?

Monroe was the last president to come from the generation that had taken part in the birth of our nation. Like those other Virginian presidents, he came from a well-to-do family. He was a college student when fighting broke out between the colonies and Great Britain. He promptly left his studies and joined General Washington's army. He fought in a number of important battles.

President James Monroe

After the war, Monroe studied law and then held a number of important jobs in the national government. He was one of the people President Jefferson sent to France to buy Louisiana. He later served as Madison's secretary of state.

Much about James Monroe seemed old-fashioned. He even dressed in an old-fashioned way, wearing knee pants long after most men had switched to trousers. He wore shoes with silver buckles and wore his hair in a pigtail, both of which had gone out of style many years before.

Still, people seemed to like Monroe. Perhaps they felt comfortable with him. Perhaps it was because he didn't lecture them. Like those earlier presidents, he knew a lot about farming. Like them, he loved books and learning. And like them, he believed in duty to his community and his country. Also, everyone agreed that he was as honest as the day is long. That's a lot of things to like about a person.

When Monroe ran for reelection in 1820, no one ran against him. However, that wasn't just because he was well-liked. It was because of an important change in the political parties. The Federalists had not won an election since John Adams was president, before 1800. Over the years, the Federalist Party had become less and less popular. Many Federalists had opposed the War of 1812, and some even sounded like they'd be happier if the union of states broke up.

That's not a good way to win elections. When Monroe ran for his first term, the Federalist Party wasn't able to offer much opposition. By the time he ran for a second term, the Federalist Party was very much in decline.

Spain Loses Power and Colonies

Spain once had the largest **colonial empire** in the world. The Spanish had controlled all of Central America, nearly all of South America, and a big chunk of North America as well. But those days were long gone. In the 1800s, Spain was a weaker nation. Many of its colonies in the Americas were overthrowing Spanish rule.

> **Vocabulary**
>
> **"colonial empire,"** (phrase) a group of countries or territories that are controlled by people from another country

Spain still claimed Florida. But it had only a handful of settlements there, and it was clear there would never be more. Most of Florida was home to the Seminoles, a large group of Native Americans. Sometimes Seminoles would cross the border into the state of Georgia and raid Georgians' farms. The Spanish government had promised to prevent those raids. It did not, however, have nearly enough soldiers in Florida to do so. Plantation owners in Southern states were also upset. Their enslaved workers often ran away to Florida—a place that represented freedom. Because Florida was not part of the United States, they could not get them back.

After another Seminole raid into Georgia, President Monroe sent General Andrew Jackson to deal with them. Jackson's army pursued the Seminoles into Florida, battled them, and burned their villages and crops. Jackson also marched into several of the Spanish forts and took them over.

General Jackson had gone much farther than he was supposed to, and Spain protested. President Monroe ordered Jackson to pull his forces out of Florida. But by then, everyone could see how weak Spain was. America knew that Spain could not hope to hang on to Florida. Spain knew it, too.

Monroe's secretary of state was John Quincy Adams, son of the second president of the United States. Adams offered Spain $5 million for Florida, and Spain accepted. In 1821, Florida was officially added to the ever-growing United States.

By that time, nearly all of Spain's colonies had won their independence. Many of these newly independent nations, such as Argentina and Bolivia in South America, looked to the United States as an example of how to set up new governments. They wrote constitutions that used many of the same ideas, and even some of the

Despite the destruction of their villages and crops, the Seminoles were not defeated. Even after two wars with the U.S. Army and relocation to Indian Territory, the Seminoles never admitted defeat!

same words, as the U.S. Constitution. That made Americans feel good. It is always a nice feeling when someone wants to imitate you. The vision of the founders that they would be a "city upon a hill," a beacon of freedom, a republic that protected liberties was coming true. For their part, North Americans were enthusiastic about independence in South America. They even named some towns after newly liberated South American countries—for example Peru, Illinois.

Some European countries, though, were not happy about this turn of events. They did not want their own colonies thinking about independence. Perhaps, they thought, the best way to keep that from happening would be to help Spain get back its South American colonies.

Now it was America's turn to be unhappy. President Monroe and Secretary of State Adams wanted each new nation to be able to shape its own future. They believed it was important for the United States to take a strong stand against any interference in the Americas from European countries.

So in 1823 at Secretary of State Adams's suggestion, President Monroe declared that European countries must not try to regain control of Spain's colonies. The United States was not interfering in Europe's affairs, said Monroe, so Europe should not interfere with the affairs of the Western Hemisphere. President Monroe's message to Europe was sweet and simple: Hands off! This policy became known as the **Monroe Doctrine**.

> **Vocabulary**
>
> **Monroe Doctrine,** n. a statement of U.S. foreign policy that opposed European involvement in the Western Hemisphere

President John Quincy Adams

You'll remember that the only party left by this time was the Democratic-Republican Party, or just the Republican Party, as it was usually called by then. The Federalist Party had withered away. Don't think for a minute, though, that there weren't any more contests for the presidency. The Republicans split into several different groups, and new parties were formed. In 1824, four candidates competed for the presidency. Two of them were Andrew Jackson and John Quincy Adams. The election was very close, but Adams won, even though many of Jackson's supporters charged—wrongly—that he had won unfairly.

John Quincy Adams certainly was well-trained for the presidency. His parents, John and Abigail Adams, saw to it that he was well-educated. He could translate Greek, and he could speak French. When he was only fourteen years old, he was already serving his

country as a secretary to the U.S. ambassador to Russia. After that, he continued to serve his country in one important job after another. As you have read, he was President Monroe's secretary of state.

During all those years, and as president too, John Quincy Adams followed a rigorous daily routine. He rose at 5:00 a.m. He built a fire in the fireplace, read his Bible, and then went out to the

John Quincy Adams became the nation's sixth president.

Potomac River and swam and bathed. After that, he was ready to start his workday.

Adams was very bright, hardworking, and honest. Like his father, he believed in doing what was right, not just what was popular. And he had many good ideas, including building a national university and better roads to tie the nation together.

Unfortunately, he was unable to get support for these ideas. In part, that was because many members of Congress still supported Andrew Jackson and opposed anything that Adams wanted. They thought the federal government spending money on roads and bridges was unconstitutional. It also was because other congressmen just did not agree with his ideas. And finally, it was because John Quincy Adams did not believe the president should try to persuade members of Congress to follow him. He believed the president should just present ideas, and then it was up to Congress to consider them. But that's really not the way to be a successful president.

Even if Adams tried to persuade members of Congress to support his ideas, he probably would not have been good at it. He was not an easy man to warm up to.

So even though John Quincy Adams had great training and great ability, he did not become a great president. Like his father, he was unable to get reelected. When he ran for a second term, he was again opposed by Andrew Jackson. This time, Jackson won.

Chapter 9
Jackson and the Common Man

A Different President "I never saw anything like it before," wrote an amazed U.S. senator. Neither had anyone else. The senator was writing about the crowds in Washington, D.C., on March 4, 1829. That was the day Andrew Jackson took the oath of office as president of the United States.

The Big Question

Why was the election of Andrew Jackson important to ordinary Americans?

Twenty thousand Americans—farmers, frontier people, ordinary folks from towns and countryside—flocked to the capital to witness the event. And to celebrate, too. After Jackson took the oath at the Capitol, the crowds followed him to the White House. In they went, walking across the carpeted floors in muddy boots, standing on chairs and furniture to get a good look at their president. Dishes were broken and punch bowls knocked over as people helped themselves to refreshments. A woman who was there reported later that "those who got in could not get out by the door again, but had to scramble out the windows."

Andrew Jackson

President Jackson himself had to escape by a side door. He spent his first night as president at a hotel. Someone finally got an idea for getting the crowd to leave the White House. They carried the tubs of punch out to the lawn. The people followed.

What happened at the White House that day was a result of an important change that had occurred in the United States. The American people had long been choosing representatives to make their laws and to carry them out. In the early years, however, only adult white males who owned property could vote.

Rise of the Common Man

As time went on, Americans began to ask why it was necessary to own property to vote. Those questions were part of a larger democratic spirit that had been sweeping America since the early 1800s.

Where did this new democratic spirit come from? Partly from the West. People who moved to the frontier were used to relying on themselves and their neighbors. They

> **Vocabulary**
>
> **consent,** n. approval or agreement

were used to making their own decisions. They expected to make decisions about who would serve in their governments and who would give **consent** to laws.

The new democratic spirit also came from eastern cities. Many workers in the cities did not have much money or property. However, they felt they should have as much say in government as property owners did.

As a result, by the late 1820s, except in a handful of states, the laws were changed. *All* adult white males could vote, whether they owned property or not. This change has been called "the rise of the **common man**."

Of course if only white males could vote, that still left out a lot of people. It left out women. It left out Native Americans. It left out African Americans—although five states did allow free African Americans to vote. With all those people left out, the changes of the early 1800s do not seem so great today. In fact, though, they were a big step toward greater democracy in America.

There was more democracy and a higher number of voters in the United States than in any other country in the world at that time.

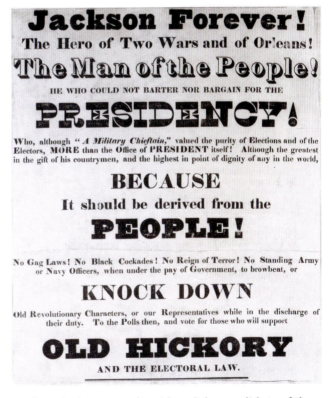

A spirit of equality accompanied the growth of democracy. Americans believed that every person was as good as the next. Earlier, when Americans voted for their representatives in government, they

Andrew Jackson was considered the candidate of the common man.

usually chose people who were well-educated and owned property. These were the people who were considered leaders. Now, though, citizens began to ask why ordinary Americans like themselves could not do just as good a job running the country.

When voting for president, they no longer looked for philosophers like Thomas Jefferson or James Madison. They wanted a person who had things in common with themselves. They liked the idea of a president who had started life as a common person.

For many Americans, Andrew Jackson was just such a person. He was born in a log cabin on the frontier. His father died two months before he was born. His mother died when he was fourteen. Andrew had to make his own way in life. He had a little schooling. As an adult, however, he became a lawyer. (In those days, there were no special law schools. You could become a lawyer by studying with someone who was already a lawyer.) Jackson also served as a judge. He also was a member of Congress for a short time. He bought land in Tennessee and raised tobacco and cotton.

Most Americans, though, knew Andrew Jackson as a soldier. They remembered him as the hero of the Battle of New Orleans. They had cheered when General Jackson helped the United States gain Florida. Andrew Jackson was the first president from the West. Ordinary Americans thought of Jackson as one of them. They felt close enough to call him Andy or to refer to him by his nickname, "Old Hickory." That was a fitting name since hickory trees were the hardest and strongest of trees from the woods of Tennessee. (For many years, baseball bats were made of hickory.) Can you imagine anyone calling President Washington "Georgie"

Americans remembered Andrew Jackson as the hero of the Battle of New Orleans.

or President Jefferson "Tommy"? So you see, those thousands of people who filled Washington, D.C., to celebrate Jackson's victory were also celebrating their own triumph.

Even though President Jackson was seen as a "man of the people," he exercised his presidential powers strongly. He **vetoed** a congressional bill for a renewal of the national bank because he thought it was unconstitutional. South Carolina created a controversy when it said it would not collect a tariff, or tax on imports, that they believed would hurt the South. Indeed, South Carolina argued that it possessed the right to nullify or veto a national law within its own borders. Jackson threatened to use the army to force the state to collect the tax. Eventually, the federal government and South Carolina compromised on a new tax. But Jackson strongly used the powers of his office.

Jackson and Native Americans

Jackson was a successful president in many ways. But his treatment of Native Americans was terrible, and many criticized him for his ruthlessness.

Although most eastern Native Americans had already been forced to move west across the Mississippi River, a number of nations

Andrew Jackson signed the Indian Removal Act in 1830. This led to the forceful removal of Native Americans from their land over a period of time. The Cherokee, forced from their homeland, had to leave behind homes, farms, and stores. This forceful removal became known as the Trail of Tears because many people died on the way to Oklahoma.

remained in the East. White settlers wanted Native American land for farming, and Jackson and Congress were determined that they should have it.

In 1830, Congress passed the Indian Removal Act. This law allowed the federal government to force the remaining Native Americans out of the eastern United States. They had to move to land set aside for them in present-day Oklahoma.

Five tribes—the Cherokee, Choctaw, Chickasaw, Creek (Muskogee), and Seminole—resisted, but the U.S. Army was too much for them. Finally, they moved. By the time Andrew Jackson left the presidency, nearly all Native Americans had been forced to move west of the Mississippi River. This was not an honorable time in U.S. history, and for many Native Americans it was a tragedy.

Seven Presidents

Washington, Adams, Jefferson, Madison, Monroe, Quincy Adams, and Jackson: these were America's first presidents. In personality, they differed greatly, some as much as night and day. They did not all share the same vision of what the America of the future should be. But these seven presidents were alike in several important ways. Each was dedicated to helping the new country grow and to helping its people prosper. Each did everything he could to make the country safe from possible enemies. Each was determined to bring success to the world's first great experiment in republican government. In all these ways, they succeeded. The United States was fortunate to have their leadership.

Glossary

A

administration, n. a group of people responsible for carrying out the day-to-day workings of an organization **(14)**

architect, n. a person who designs buildings **(31)**

Articles of Confederation, n. the first plan of government of the United States; replaced by the U.S. Constitution in 1789 **(5)**

B

Bill of Rights, n. the first ten amendments to the U.S. Constitution, which list specific rights that must be protected **(13)**

boardinghouse, n. a place to stay or live that also provides meals **(33)**

C

"colonial empire," (phrase) a group of countries or territories that are controlled by people from another country **(61)**

"common man," (phrase) an ordinary person; someone who is not a member of the wealthy or ruling classes **(69)**

consent, n. approval or agreement **(68)**

currency, n. a system of money **(18)**

D

delegate, n. a representative **(5)**

diverse, adj. having many different types or parts **(17)**

E

Electoral College, n. a group of representatives who elect the president and vice president, based on the popular vote in each state **(36)**

embargo, n. a government order that limits or stops trade **(49)**

executive, adj. having the power to carry out and enforce laws **(10)**

F

frontier, n. where newly settled areas meet unsettled, but not necessarily uninhabited, areas **(19)**

frontiersmen, n. people who live in an unsettled area or the wilderness **(56)**

furnace, n. a device or machine that produces heat **(35)**

I

impressment, n. the act of seizing seamen to serve against their will as sailors in a navy **(48)**

J

judicial, adj. having the power to decide questions of law **(10)**

L

legislative, adj. having the power to make laws **(10)**

M

merchant ship, n. a ship that transports goods for sale or trade **(48)**

militia, n. a group of armed citizens prepared for military service at any time **(51)**

Monroe Doctrine, n. a statement of U.S. foreign policy that opposed European involvement in the Western Hemisphere **(63)**

moral, adj. relating to ideas of right and wrong **(24)**

O

oath of office, n. a promise made by a government official to obey the law and fulfill the responsibilities of his or her job **(7)**

P

philosopher, n. a thinker; a person who seeks wisdom and knowledge **(38)**

precedent, n. an example for future actions or decisions (8)

R

rampart, n. a thick wall built for protection (55)

ratify, v. to approve (6)

republic, n. a government in which people elect representatives to rule for them (4)

resignation, n. the act of stepping down from or leaving a job (4)

S

secretary of state, n. the U.S. government official in charge of helping the president in his dealings with foreign countries (50)

serve, v. to work for one's country, as a government official or in the military (5)

stable, adj. likely to stay the same and not change (17)

surveyor, n. a person who measures the shape, size, and features of an area of land (30)

T

tax, n. money that people are required to pay to support the workings of the government (10)

U

unalienable, adj. unable to be taken away or denied (40)

V

veto, v. to reject or refuse to approve a law (71)

vote, n. an official choice made by a person through casting a ballot, raising a hand, or speaking aloud (19)

American Reformers

Table of Contents

American Reformers
Reader
Core Knowledge History and Geography™

Chapter 1
Springtime of Reform

Making Life Better How can we make life better for people less fortunate than ourselves? Chances are you have heard that question

The Big Question

What was the temperance movement?

many times. You have probably thought about it. Maybe you have shared your ideas on that subject with others. People who spend a lot of time and effort trying to make things better are called reformers.

Vocabulary

active, adj. busy; doing something

There have always been reformers in America, more at some times in our history than at others. The 1830s and 1840s were an especially **active** time for reformers. In this land of growing democracy and equality, Americans believed that everything was possible.

Thousands of Americans took part in reform movements. They believed they could make life fairer by changing attitudes and changing laws. They believed that doing these things would make the United States a better country.

Temperance reformers wanted people to stop drinking so much alcohol.

WOMANS HOLY WAR.

The Temperance Movement

One group of reformers was concerned about people who drank too much alcohol. You probably know that this is still a problem today. Believe it or not, it was even worse in the early 1800s. Americans then drank *three times* as much alcohol per person as they do today.

Most heavy drinkers were grown men, but a large number were teenagers. On the frontier, women also drank heavily. Drinking ruined many homes and many lives. It contributed to poverty and crime.

The problem of heavy drinking gave rise to one of the important reform movements of the 1800s, the **temperance** movement. Temperance means drinking little alcohol, or none at all. Reformers believed that if people gave up alcohol, their lives would improve and their families would be saved from pain and poverty.

Reformers delivered their message in many different ways. They wrote songs, put on plays, handed out pamphlets, and delivered sermons in church. They organized huge parades of children who carried banners begging grown-ups to stop drinking. (Reformers called the children who paraded the Cold Water Army. Can you see why?) Reformers also got drinkers to sign a **pledge**, or promise, that they would stop, or at least reduce, their drinking. More than one million people took the pledge.

> **Vocabulary**
>
> **temperance,** n. the practice of drinking little or no alcohol
>
> **pledge,** n. a promise

Temperance reformers used children to convince adults to take the temperance pledge.

As the years passed, some people who signed the pledge did start drinking again. Nevertheless, the temperance movement was successful. In just ten years, Americans were drinking less than half as much alcohol as before.

Chapter 2
Treating Mental Illnesses

Dorothea Dix Temperance reformers tried to improve people's lives by getting them to change their own behavior. Other reformers tried to help people who had mental illnesses. These reformers believed that others would help if they only knew about the sad conditions in which these people lived.

The Big Question
....
How did Dorothea Dix change the treatment of people with mental illnesses?

Dorothea Dix was one of those reformers. She worked very hard to get kinder treatment for people with mental health problems. Dix had not always been a reformer. She started teaching school in Boston at the age of fourteen—you could do that in those days. After working for twenty-five years, she became ill and had to stop. Soon after, a friend asked if she could teach a Sunday school class for women prisoners in the East Cambridge jail, near Boston.

Dix went. What she saw changed her life. Of course, she had expected to find women charged with committing crimes, and she did. But she was completely unprepared to find inmates suffering from serious mental illnesses. They were clothed in rags and kept in a single filthy, unheated room.

These people had committed no crime. They were simply ill. In those days, there were no effective treatments for mental illness. Most towns and cities just wanted these people out of the way. A few states had hospitals

Dorothea Dix worked to improve care for people who suffered from mental illnesses.

called **asylums**. Massachusetts was one of them, thanks to the efforts of a reformer named Horace Mann. (You will meet Horace Mann again when you read about another important reform.) But the Massachusetts hospital was a small one. Most states just put people with mental health problems in jails or in almshouses. Almshouses were places where people who were extremely poor were sent to live. Often they were just locked up and forgotten. Their "keepers" often treated them with great cruelty.

A Life's Work

The experience at the prison upset Dorothea Dix so much that she spent the rest of her life working to improve conditions for people with mental illnesses. She started by visiting jails and almshouses all over the state. She took careful notes on the conditions she found. In one of her notebooks she wrote that people were held "in *cages, closets, cellars, stalls, pens!*" "*They were chained naked, beaten with rods, and lashed [whipped] into obedience!*"

Dix knew that only the state government could change these conditions. She arranged to speak before the Massachusetts **state legislature**. She began:

> I come to present the strong claims of suffering humanity. I come to place before the Legislature of Massachusetts the conditions of the miserable, the **desolate**, the outcast. I come as the **advocate** of helpless, forgotten, insane . . . men and women, . . . wretched in our prisons, and more wretched in our almshouses.

Then, she described the hopeless conditions she had found.

The people in charge of the jails and almshouses denied everything. They accused Dix of making up lies. But Dorothea Dix's evidence was so convincing that the legislators believed her. The lawmakers agreed to make the state hospital bigger so that it could take in more people.

Dix then carried her work to other states. She went as far west as Illinois and as far south as Alabama. Almost none of those states had so much as one hospital for people with mental health issues. Wherever she went, Dix followed the same plan that had worked in Massachusetts. She visited as many jails and almshouses as she could. She filled her notebooks with information about the treatment of people with mental health problems in that state. Then, she presented her findings to the public and the state legislature. Finally, she recommended that the legislature create special hospitals where trained people would treat mental health patients as human beings instead of as animals.

Altogether, Dorothea Dix visited more than eight hundred jails and almshouses. She persuaded more than a dozen states to improve care for mental health patients. In the forty years after Dix visited that jail in East Cambridge, 110 new mental health hospitals were built in the United States. Most of the credit for that belongs to the brave and determined reformer, Dorothea Dix.

Chapter 3
Educating for Democracy

School for Everyone When you read about Dorothea Dix, you met Horace Mann. He was the person who got the state of Massachusetts to build the first hospital for mental health patients. He became most famous, though, for another great reform. He led the movement to provide free public school education for all.

The Big Question

Why did Horace Mann want to give all children the right to an education?

Vocabulary

tutor, n. a teacher who teaches only one student, usually in the student's home

In Horace Mann's time, there were few free public schools outside New England. These schools were mainly for poor children. But the schools were usually as poor as the children they served. Wealthy families either hired private **tutors** for their children or sent them to private schools. Most families, though, were in the middle—not poor, not wealthy. What about those children? Their parents either taught them at home or joined with other parents and hired someone to teach them.

Horace Mann led the campaign for public schools.

Even in New England, where the taxpayers provided free public education, the schools were not very good. Take Massachusetts, for example. In many towns, the school "year" was only two months long. School buildings were often run down and unheated. Teachers had no training for the difficult tasks they had to do. (That's how Dorothea Dix could become a teacher at age fourteen.) As in other states, wealthy families in Massachusetts paid for private tutors or private schools.

As a boy, Horace Mann went to one of those two-months-a-year schools. In later years, he studied on his own. He became a lawyer and was elected to the Massachusetts state legislature. In the legislature, and later as a state official, he worked to provide a good education for every child in the state.

Mann spoke at many public meetings to get support for his ideas. He told his listeners how education could improve the lives of their children. He told them education would help their children get better jobs than their parents had. He told them that Thomas Jefferson believed that only an educated people could expect to remain free. He told them that democracy and education go hand in hand. For a democracy to succeed, all children—not just the children of the wealthy—must be educated to become good citizens and wise voters.

Making a Difference

Many different people supported Mann's ideas. Business people needed workers who could read, write, and do math. Working people hoped that education would lead to a better life for their children. Those who had thought about how to preserve freedom and democracy in America also knew that Mann was right. All these people realized that the best hope for providing all children with a good education was free public schools.

But not everyone agreed. Some said that if you "give away" education to the children of the poor, they would grow up lazy. Others grumbled about paying taxes to educate other people's children. Still, most Americans agreed that spending money to educate children was a wise investment for the whole country.

Under Horace Mann's leadership, the state of Massachusetts created schools for training teachers. The state provided enough money to pay for six months of school each year for all boys and girls. It divided schools into grades instead of having children of all ages trying to learn different things in the same classroom. It also passed a law saying that all children must attend a school.

Massachusetts became a model for other states. Many states asked Horace Mann to help them make the same school reforms.

Most northern and western states started free public schools. (Southern states did not do the same until many years later.) Today, Horace Mann is known as the Father of the American Public School.

Massachusetts public schools became an inspiration to other states.

Chapter 4
Abolitionism

The Crusade Against Slavery

The largest and most emotionally charged reform movement of the 1800s was the abolitionist movement. This was the movement to end to slavery in the United States.

The Big Question

What difficulties did the abolitionists face as they worked to abolish slavery?

Many Americans came to believe that enslaving people was wrong.

Many Americans were coming to believe that slavery was wrong. "All men are created equal," says the Declaration of Independence. All have the **unalienable rights** to life and to liberty. All of our early presidents— Washington, Adams, Jefferson, Madison, Monroe—felt that slavery was wrong and believed it would end in time. But saying that slavery is wrong was one thing. Actually doing something to **abolish** it was another. In fact, all of those early presidents, except John Adams, owned slaves themselves. Several northern states passed laws to end slavery. But no Southern state did, and that is where most enslaved people lived.

Some slave owners in the South freed their enslaved workers. One slave owner in North Carolina gave these four reasons for doing so:

> Reason the first: every human being . . . is entitled to freedom.

> Reason the second: my **conscience** condemns me for keeping them in slavery.

> Reason the third: the **golden rule** directs us to do unto every human creature, as we would wish to be done unto.

> Reason the fourth and last: I wish to die with a clear conscience that I may not be ashamed to appear before my master in a future world.

But these were all individual deeds. These owners were only a small minority of all slave owners. The flame of antislavery feeling never burned strongly in the South, and eventually died out.

Abolitionists wanted to light that flame again. Most abolitionists were religious people. They believed that slavery was not just wrong but a great sin in the eyes of God. They thought the way to end slavery was to appeal to the conscience of slave owners. They thought that once masters understood how sinful it was for one person to own another, they would give up their enslaved workers, just the way that North Carolina slaveholder did.

Things did not work out as they hoped. Slave owners were not interested in the abolitionists' message. Some of them even said that enslaved people benefited from slavery!

Abolitionists changed their plan. They began educating Northerners on the evils of slavery. They formed antislavery organizations. They handed out more than a million pamphlets. They gave public lectures.

William Lloyd Garrison was one of the leading abolitionists. Garrison published an abolitionist newspaper called *The Liberator*. He also started the American Anti-Slavery Society, which was the main organization of abolitionist reformers. Frederick Douglass was another important abolitionist. Douglass had escaped from slavery. When he spoke about slavery, his listeners knew that he spoke from experience. Douglass later wrote a book about his life as an enslaved person and his escape. His book is called *Narrative of the Life of Frederick Douglass, an American Slave*. He, too, published an abolitionist newspaper.

William Lloyd Garrison used his newspaper *The Liberator* to inform people about the evils of slavery.

At first, there were just a few abolitionists. Only a few thousand people in the whole country bought *The Liberator*. Even in the North, where most people did not like slavery, abolitionists were not popular. That is because abolitionists were not just saying they did not like slavery. They were saying that the country should *do* something about it—abolish it, not at some time in the future but now.

Abolitionists believed deeply in their cause. They kept working to achieve freedom for enslaved people. In public meetings, they described the cruel treatment of enslaved workers, which included beatings and whippings. They spoke of husbands being separated from wives and of children being sold and separated from their parents. In time, a growing number of people came

94

to understand the true horrors of slavery. Some came over to the abolitionists' side and supported their arguments. And even those who did not come all the way over believed more strongly than ever that slavery was evil and must not be allowed to spread.

Still, it was not until the end of the Civil War in 1865, when Constitutional amendments were passed, that the abolitionists saw their goal become a reality.

Despite the testimony of formerly enslaved people, such as Frederick Douglass, abolitionists struggled to win support for their goal.

Chapter 5
Women and the Fight for Equality

Women Speak Out Sisters Angelina and Sarah Grimké grew up in South Carolina. They lived with slavery, and they hated it. They felt so strongly about it that they left the South.

The Big Question

What did the anti-slavery movement reveal about the rights of women?

In the 1830s, the Grimké sisters began giving talks about plantation life and slavery to audiences of men and women in northern towns and cities. Many people were shocked to hear the sisters lecture on the evils of slavery. But it was not *what* the sisters said that shocked them. It was the fact that these women were speaking to the public *at all*. At that time women, like children, were supposed to be seen and not heard. Most men agreed with the old saying, "A woman's place is in the home." Women might speak to groups of other women. But they should not speak at public meetings when men were in the audience. That role belonged to men only.

Angelina and Sarah Grimké were often criticized for their work as abolitionists.

That is what the world was like for women in the first half of the 1800s. It was just one of the ways that women lacked **equal rights**. Women also lacked equal opportunity in education. In those days, few people—male or female—got more than a few years of schooling. But a man was much more likely to finish high school or go to college than a woman was. You rarely heard of a woman who became a doctor or a lawyer. And when women did work, they usually earned very low wages.

There is more. In most states, when a woman married, everything she owned, even money or property given to her by her parents, became the property of her husband. If she worked, her earnings belonged to her husband. If parents divorced, it was usually the father, not the mother, who got the children. That was the law. Because women could not vote or hold government **office**, the laws would not be changed unless men voted to change them. In time, men did. But the changes were few, and they came very slowly.

Sarah Grimké became so angry about these laws and attitudes, she wrote a pamphlet to express her outrage. "Men and women are CREATED EQUAL," she wrote. She went on to say:

Whatever is *right* for man to do, is *right* for woman. . . . All I ask of [men] is, that they will take their feet from off our necks and permit us to stand upright on that ground which God designed us to occupy.

Those were very angry words, but you can certainly understand why Sarah Grimké wrote them.

You might think that men who were reformers would have a different attitude about women. Some did, but not most. One woman who joined a temperance organization found that men held all the offices and made all the speeches. She was told that "the sisters were not invited there to speak but to listen and learn." Women in the antislavery movement were treated the same way, even though they made up more than half of its members. **Ministers** who strongly supported abolition refused to allow women to speak at antislavery meetings in their churches.

That was the attitude in most parts of the world. Women delegates to a World Anti-Slavery **Convention** in London, England, were not allowed to take part in the meeting. They could only watch from a balcony. So you see, even when working for the cause of freedom, women were expected to take a back seat—or in this case, an upstairs seat—to men.

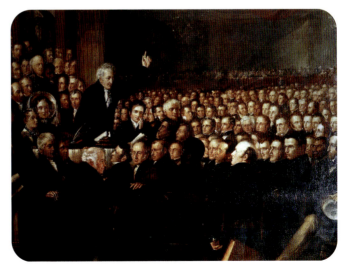

At the World Anti-Slavery Convention in 1841, women were not allowed in the main audience.

Chapter 6
The Seneca Falls Convention

A Women's Rights Convention On July 14, 1848, this notice appeared in the *Seneca Country Courier* newspaper: "Woman's Rights Convention: A Convention to discuss the social, civil, and religious conditions and rights of woman will be held in the Wesleyan Chapel, at Seneca Falls, N.Y."

The Big Question

Why might some newspapers have made fun of the women's movement and its demands?

Few would have guessed that this short announcement would start one of the biggest reform movements in U.S. history.

The idea for a women's rights convention had been born eight years earlier. You remember the World Anti-Slavery Convention in London? When women delegates were told they could watch from the balcony but not take part? Two of the women sitting in that balcony were Lucretia Mott and Elizabeth Cady Stanton.

Mott and Stanton

Lucretia Mott and her husband, James, were active in many of the reform movements of the day. Mott once organized a campaign asking

THE FIRST CONVENTION

EVER CALLED TO DISCUSS THE

Civil and Political Rights of Women,

SENECA FALLS, N. Y., JULY 19, 20, 1848.

WOMAN'S RIGHTS CONVENTION.

A Convention to discuss the social, civil, and religious condition and rights of woman will be held in the Wesleyan Chapel, at Seneca Falls, N. Y., on Wednesday and Thursday, the 19th and 20th of July current; commencing at 10 o'clock A. M. During the first day the meeting will be exclusively for women, who are earnestly invited to attend. The public generally are invited to be present on the second day, when Lucretia Mott, of Philadelphia, and other ladies and gentlemen, will address the Convention.*

---

* This call was published in the *Seneca County Courier*, July 14, 1848, without any signatures. The movers of this Convention, who drafted the call, the declaration and resolutions were Elizabeth Cady Stanton, Lucretia Mott, Martha C. Wright, Mary Ann McClintock, and Jane C. Hunt.

In 1848, a women's rights convention was held in Seneca Falls, New York.

people not to buy products made or raised by enslaved workers. Those products included cotton clothing, sugar, and rice. She hoped that would convince plantation owners to give up slavery.

Still, despite her reform work, Mott always felt that as a woman she did not receive the same level of respect as a man. She later said that women's rights were "the most important question of my life from a very early day."

As for Elizabeth Cady, she learned about the unequal treatment of women very early in life. Her father was a lawyer and a judge. "Oh, my daughter," he said on one occasion, "I wish you were a boy." As a girl, Elizabeth could never become a lawyer like her father.

Cady resolved to show her father that she was as good as a boy. She learned to play games, such as chess, that men said were beyond the mental powers of girls and women. She studied Greek and Latin. She studied mathematics. Still, no matter how well she did, she could not go to college. Colleges were for men only. Cady had to attend a school for women in Troy, New York, instead.

After graduating, Cady became active in a number of reform movements. She soon met Henry B. Stanton, a leader in the antislavery movement. The two decided to marry. In those days, women promised to "love, honor, and obey" their husbands in the marriage vow. Elizabeth Cady insisted on removing the word *obey*. The Stantons spent their honeymoon in London, England, where they attended the World Anti-Slavery Convention.

Lucretia Mott was a good deal older than Elizabeth Cady Stanton. The two had never met before the London meeting. Both were angered by their treatment. By the time they left London, they had promised each other to hold a convention on women's rights in the United States.

Seneca Falls

For eight years, nothing came of the promise. Elizabeth Cady Stanton was busy raising a family. Lucretia Mott was involved in other activities. Then on July 13, 1848, Mott visited the Stanton's home in Seneca Falls, New York. That afternoon over a cup of tea, Stanton, Mott, and three local women decided to hold the long-delayed convention. They would have it in Seneca Falls six days from that day.

On July 19, two hundred women, and even some men, showed up at the Wesleyan Chapel. On the second day, a larger crowd of women and men attended. Among them was the abolitionist Frederick Douglass.

> **Vocabulary**
>
> **sentiment,** n. a thought or feeling

Elizabeth Cady Stanton read aloud a Declaration of **Sentiments** she had written. The Declaration's first words echoed another famous declaration: "We hold these truths to be self-evident: that all men and women are created equal." Stanton went on to list fifteen ways that women were treated unequally.

Women, along with some male supporters, gathered at Seneca Falls to hold a convention on women's rights.

At the end of the Declaration, Elizabeth Cady Stanton shocked the audience. She demanded that women be given the right to vote. For some reformers, that was going too far. Lucretia Mott tried to discourage her friend. Demanding the vote "will make us look ridiculous," she said. "We must go slowly." But Mott eventually agreed. So did a majority of the convention.

Today, it is hard to imagine anyone disagreeing with the goals of the Seneca Falls Convention. However, that was a different time. The few newspapers that paid attention to the meeting made fun of it. One laughed at the women's demands to vote, become lawyers, and keep their own property. While they were at it, said the newspaper, they should have demanded that men "wash dishes, . . . handle the broom, darn stockings, . . . wear trinkets, [and] look beautiful."

None of this ridicule stopped the women's movement. After the Seneca Falls meeting, women in a half-dozen other states organized similar meetings.

More Heroes

The movement for women's rights had other **heroines** besides Elizabeth Cady Stanton and Lucretia Mott. There was Lucy Stone, the first American woman to deliver a public lecture on women's rights. When Lucy Stone married, she kept her own name.

> **Vocabulary**
>
> **heroine,** n. a brave or admired woman; a female hero

There was Elizabeth Blackwell. She became the first woman graduate of a medical college.

Then there was Amelia Bloomer. She wore large, roomy trousers with a short skirt over them because they were more comfortable than the heavy dresses women were expected to wear.

There was also a woman named Sojourner Truth. Nearly six feet tall and wearing a white turban, Sojourner Truth became a familiar person at public meetings on women's rights. She was a former enslaved worker, and she could not read or write. But she could speak. To those who said women were weak, Sojourner said, "I have as much muscle as any man, and can do as much work as any man. I have plowed and **reaped** and **husked** and chopped and mowed, and can any man do more than that?" When Sojourner Truth was speaking at a different convention, a few rowdy men showed up to jeer. Sojourner Truth had these words for them: "I am sorry to see [some men] so short-minded. But we'll have our rights; see if we don't; and you can't stop us from them; see if you can. You may hiss as much as you like, but it is comin'."

In 1851, in Akron, Ohio, Sojourner Truth delivered her famous "Ain't I a Woman?" speech.

Sojourner Truth was right. But, it would be some time before it happened.

Additional Resources: Reform and Civil Rights—The Continuing Story

The Case of John Lewis

As you read, the early 1800s were busy years for reformers and reform movements. Reformers, such as Dorothea Dix and Horace Mann, called for changes and new laws. In many cases, they were successful.

The Big Question

What was the civil rights movement of the 1950s–1960s, and what did it accomplish?

However, this was not the *only* time in American history when reformers called for changes. In fact, there have *always* been reformers in America.

Some reformers succeeded in changing the nation and its laws. Others failed. But many people would argue that part of what makes America a great country is that lawmakers have often listened to reformers— though there have been times when they did not. Throughout our history many new laws have been passed, and many changes have been made.

In the 1950s and 1960s, many reformers fought for fair treatment of African Americans. African people were brought to America in the 1600s and 1700s as enslaved workers. They and their descendants were forced to work in houses and on plantations. They had no political rights. They could be bought or sold. They could be whipped for disobeying their masters.

Slavery was outlawed in the 1860s, after the Civil War. However, this did not mean that African Americans were treated equally. In many places, especially in some southern states, African Americans were not treated equally. They were not allowed to use the same restrooms or eat in the same restaurants as white Americans. They were sent to separate schools. Often they were not allowed to vote. And because they could not vote, they could not pick lawmakers who might be willing to pass new laws. In all of these ways, African Americans were segregated—that is, kept apart. They were kept apart from white people, who had almost all of the political power and made the laws.

Many men and women spoke out against segregation. You may have learned about Martin Luther King Jr. He was an African American who spoke out against segregation and fought for equal rights for African Americans. There were also many other Americans who worked for reform and civil rights. One you may not have heard about is John Lewis.

John Lewis was born and raised in Alabama, the son of poor farmers. He did well in school and was admitted to Fisk University in Nashville, Tennessee. Fisk is a university for African Americans.

At Fisk, Lewis was drawn into the civil rights movement. He joined with other students to stage a series of protests called "sit-ins."

John Lewis was a leader of the 1960s civil rights movement. Today, he is a U.S. congressman.

The idea was that African American students would sit down at lunch counters in Nashville that were reserved for white people and ask to be served. If they were turned down, they would continue to sit peacefully in their seats, as a form of protest against segregation. Of course, as long as they sat in the seats, the restaurant would not be able to seat other customers. So, the owners would lose money. The students hoped they could persuade the owners to desegregate the lunch counters and serve all people side by side.

The first big sit-in in Nashville happened in February 1960. John Lewis and more than one hundred other students walked into several restaurants, sat down, and asked to be served. The servers refused, so the students sat and waited. They sat for two hours. Then, they got up and left.

In the weeks that followed, Lewis was involved in more sit-ins, and he saw them get bigger and bigger. The second sit-in attracted more than two hundred students, the third more than three hundred.

The sit-ins also attracted spectators. Some people came just to see what was going on. Others came to get involved. There were many

Peaceful protests called sit-ins were one method used by African Americans fighting for their civil rights in the 1960s.

white people in the South who had grown up with segregation. They were upset that the students were trying to change the way things were done. Some of them began taunting the students involved in the sit-ins. A few people even attacked the students.

During one sit-in, the police arrested Lewis and other protesters and hauled them off to jail. Was John Lewis ashamed? No, he was not. He actually felt excited, even joyous. He felt that it was a good thing to be thrown in jail for opposing bad laws.

John Lewis protested against segregation in many other ways. In 1965, he helped lead a protest **march** from Selma, Alabama. He and other civil rights leaders were marching to draw attention to racist laws that kept African American people in Selma and other parts of Alabama from voting.

> **Vocabulary**
>
> **march,** n. an organized walk by a group of people to support a cause

Lewis and the others marched peacefully. They sang songs and held hands. But when they crossed the bridge as they were leaving Selma, they were attacked by white police officers with clubs. Lewis was hit on the head and passed out for a few minutes. When he woke up, he found himself in a cloud of smoke. The police had fired tear gas at the protesters. Coughing and wheezing, Lewis stood and staggered back across the bridge. All around him the police continued to beat marchers—including some schoolchildren. The marchers were driven back across the bridge.

Some of the police officers probably thought that they had won a battle. But actually, they had lost. There were photographers and TV cameramen nearby, and they took pictures of the attacks. Millions of Americans saw the pictures on TV that night, and many were appalled. They could not believe what was happening. Many of them began to think it was time to pass new laws. In Washington, President Lyndon Johnson thought so, too. He decided that, if the governor and the police in Alabama would not reform themselves, he would reform them.

A new law was proposed, and it was passed: once again, American lawmakers showed themselves willing to listen to reformers. What about John Lewis? He continued protesting for a while, and then this reformer became a lawmaker himself! He has been serving in Congress ever since.

Sonia Sotomayor

In the fall of 1964, a ten-year-old girl named Sonia Sotomayor sat on the floor in her mother's New York City apartment to watch an episode of *Perry Mason*. Sotomayor loved this TV show. She loved to watch Perry Mason solve cases.

The Big Question

In your opinion, what things have contributed to Sonia Sotomayor's great success?

Mason was a lawyer who defended people charged with having committed a crime. He investigated each case like a detective. Eventually, he found a way to show that his client could not possibly have committed the crime. In many cases, he would also find the person who actually did commit the crime.

Sotomayor was fascinated by Perry Mason, but she was also fascinated by another character on the show—the judge. Sotomayor noticed that whenever Perry Mason wanted to do something in the courtroom, he had to ask the judge's permission. That seemed to mean that the judge was even more powerful and important than Perry Mason. Sonia Sotomayor felt that she might like to be a lawyer when she grew up—or possibly even a judge.

In the fall of 2009, Sotomayor sat on a swiveling leather chair in Washington, D.C., to watch two lawyers argue a case before a court. But the lawyers in this case were not TV lawyers. They were real-life lawyers. And the court was not just any court. It was the **Supreme Court** of the United States, the highest court in the country. Nine judges, called justices, filed in and took their seats in nine swiveling leather chairs. These nine justices would decide who would win the case. Sonia Sotomayor was one of them.

Sonia Sotomayor was appointed to serve on the Supreme Court of the United States by President Barack Obama.

Sotomayor had come a long way since that day in 1964 when she sat down to watch *Perry Mason*. When she was young, she spoke only a little English. Her parents were both immigrants who had moved to New York City from Puerto Rico. Puerto Rico is an island in the Caribbean where Spanish is spoken. Sotomayor's parents spoke Spanish at home, so Spanish was the language their daughter knew best.

Sonia Sotomayor's father had attended school in Puerto Rico but dropped out after third grade. Her mother stayed in school longer and became a nurse. Mrs. Sotomayor believed that the United States was a land of opportunity. She wanted her daughter to succeed. She saved money to buy Sonia an expensive set of encyclopedias called the *Encyclopedia Britannica*.

Sonia Sotomayor used those encyclopedias to learn more about lawyers and laws and courts and judges. She also learned many other things. She improved her English and worked

Sonia Sotomayor is the daughter of Puerto Rican immigrants. People from Puerto Rico enjoy celebrating their heritage.

hard in school. She won a full **scholarship** to attend Princeton University. This meant that her parents did not have to pay for her to go to college.

At first Sotomayor found college difficult. But she worked hard and became one of the best students at Princeton. After graduating from Princeton, Sotomayor went to Yale Law School, one of the top law schools in the country. Again she was awarded a scholarship.

After finishing law school, Sotomayor worked as **prosecutor** for several years. Then, she worked for a private law firm for several more years. During this time, she built a reputation as a smart, hardworking lawyer.

In 1991, Sotomayor was nominated by the president to be a federal district judge. Many people were excited when she was selected. They were excited because they respected her abilities as a lawyer and thought she would be an excellent judge. But they

Vocabulary

scholarship, n. money given to a student to help pay for a school or college

prosecutor, n. a lawyer who represents the government in criminal trials

were also excited because she was a member of the Puerto Rican immigrant community. This community had been growing rapidly and was ready to have a voice in the government of the country.

In 1930, there were only about fifty thousand Puerto Ricans in the United States. By 1990, there were almost three million. During those sixty years, millions of people came to the United States from other Spanish-speaking countries, such as Mexico, El Salvador, and the Dominican Republic. People who speak Spanish as a first or native language are known as **Hispanic**.

> **Vocabulary**
>
> **Hispanic,** adj.
> related to Spanish-speaking people or their culture

When Sotomayor took her first job as a judge, she became the first Hispanic federal judge in New York State. She was also the first Puerto Rican woman to serve as a judge in a U.S. federal court. But she was not done yet.

In 1997, Sotomayor was selected for an even more important position, as a judge on the U.S. Court of Appeals for the Second Circuit. In 2009, she was appointed to be a justice of the U.S. Supreme Court, the highest court in the United States.

Sonia Sotomayor has been serving as a Supreme Court justice ever since. If you ever go to Washington, D.C., you can see her in action. It is free to visit the Supreme Court when it is hearing a case, but you have to get in line very early.

Glossary

A

abolish, v. to end; to stop something completely (92)

active, adj. busy; doing something 78)

advocate, n. a person who supports and defends another person or group of people (84)

asylum, n. a hospital for people with mental illnesses (84)

C

conscience, n. a sense or belief a person has that a certain action is right or wrong (92)

convention, n. a formal gathering of people for a purpose (99)

D

desolate, adj. alone and hopeless (84)

E

"equal rights," (phrase) the freedoms and legal protections guaranteed to all citizens (98)

G

golden rule, n. a rule or belief in many religions that encourages people to treat others as you want to be treated (92)

H

heroine, n. a brave or admired woman; a female hero (104)

Hispanic, adj. related to Spanish-speaking people or their culture (115)

husk, v. to remove the outer covering from a plant, such as corn (105)

M

march, n. an organized walk by a group of people to support a cause (110)

minister, n. a religious leader, usually in a Protestant church (99)

O

office, n. a position of leadership or responsibility (98)

P

pledge, n. a promise (80)

prosecutor, n. a lawyer who represents the government in criminal trials (114)

R

reap, v. to cut and gather crops from where they grow (105)

S

scholarship, n. money given to a student to help pay for a school or college (114)

sentiment, n. a thought or feeling (103)

"state legislature," (phrase) the part of state government responsible for making laws for the state (84)

Supreme Court, n. the highest court in the land (113)

T

temperance, n. the practice of drinking little or no alcohol (80)

tutor, n. a teacher who teaches only one student, usually in the student's home (86)

U

"unalienable right," (phrase) a legal promise that cannot be taken away or denied (92)

CK**HG**™
Core Knowledge H**ISTORY AND** G**EOGRAPHY**™

Editorial Directors
Linda Bevilacqua and Rosie McCormick

Early Presidents
Subject Matter Expert

J. Chris Arndt, PhD

Department of History, James Madison University

Tony Williams, Senior Teaching Fellow, Bill of Rights Institute

Illustration and Photo Credits

American Reformers

Subject Matter Expert

Matthew M. Davis, PhD, University of Virginia

Tony Williams, Senior Teaching Fellow, Bill of Rights Institute

Illustration and Photo Credits